FUN FACT FILE:
WOMEN IN
HISTORY

20 FUN FACTS ABOUT PIONEER WOMEN

By Kristen Rajczak

Gareth Stevens
PUBLISHING

Please visit our website, www.garethstevens.com. For a free color catalog of all our high-quality books, call toll free 1-800-542-2595 or fax 1-877-542-2596.

Library of Congress Cataloging-in-Publication Data

Rajczak, Kristen.
20 fun facts about pioneer women / by Kristen Rajczak.
p. cm. — (Fun fact file: women in history)
Includes index.
ISBN 978-1-4824-2804-9 (pbk.)
ISBN 978-1-4824-2805-6 (6 pack)
ISBN 978-1-4824-2806-3 (library binding)
1. Women pioneers — United States — History — Juvenile literature. 2. Women pioneers — West (U.S.) —
History — Juvenile literature. 3. Frontier and pioneer life — United States — Juvenile literature. 4. Frontier and
pioneer life — West (U.S.) — Juvenile literature. 5. United States — Social life and customs — Juvenile literature.
I. Rajczak, Kristen. II. Title.
F596.R35 2016
978'.02'082—d23

First Edition

Published in 2016 by
Gareth Stevens Publishing
111 East 14th Street, Suite 349
New York, NY 10003

Designer: Andrea Davison-Bartolotta
Editor: Kristen Rajczak

Photo credits: Cover, pp. 1, 29 DEA Picture Library/DeAgostini/Getty Images; p. 5 FPG/Getty Images; p. 6
MPI/Stringer/Getty Images; p. 7 Carl Christian Anton Christensen/DEA Picture Library/Getty Images; p. 8
Hulton Archive/Stringer/Getty Images; pp. 9, 12, 16, 17 (main), 25 courtesy of the Library of Congress; p. 10
Buyenlarge/Getty Images; p. 11 Currier and Ives/Getty Images; p. 13 North Wind Picture Archives; pp. 14,
15, 23 Underwood Archives/Getty Images; p. 17 (inset) Nard the Bard/Wikimedia Commons; p. 18 Archibald
James Campbell/Wikimedia Commons; p. 19 Dick S. Ramsay Fund/Brooklyn Museum/Wikimedia Commons;
p. 20 Claudio Del Luongo/Shutterstock.com; p. 21 British Library/Wikimedia Commons; p. 22 Steve Krull/
Getty Images; p. 24 Prisma/Universal Images Group/Getty Images; p. 26 Roeder Bros./Heritage Auctions/
Wikimedia Commons; p. 28 Reservoirhill/Wikimedia Commons.

Printed in the United States of America

CPSIA compliance information: Batch #CS15GS: For further information contact Gareth Stevens, New York, New York at 1-800-542-2595.

Contents

Words in the glossary appear in **bold** type the first time they are used in the text.

The Pioneer Spirit

During the mid-1800s to late 1800s, hundreds of thousands of people traveled west to the American **frontier**. They settled in the Midwest, on the Great Plains, and even made it all the way to present-day California.

These brave settlers are often called the pioneers. A pioneer is someone who is the first to explore or settle in a new place. Pioneer women showed a special bravery on this journey. Their **perseverance** helped shape women's place in the growing United States.

Much of what we know about pioneer women comes from the women themselves! Many kept diaries that have been found and studied by **historians**.

FACT 1

Many pioneer women didn't have a choice whether to go west.

During the mid-1800s when many settlers were heading to the American frontier, women had **legal** rights similar to those of children. They left behind family and friends to follow their husband to a **homestead**.

Families often traveled with others from their town. They helped each other along the way.

FACT 2

A pioneer woman had to ask other women for help when she had to use the bathroom on the trail.

There were no toilets on the way west! One account said that when a woman had to go to the bathroom, other women stood and spread their long skirts around her so she would have privacy.

FACT 3

Women were injured on wagon trains when their skirt got stuck under the wagon wheels.

It was proper for women to wear dresses during the 1800s. However, some wore short, loose pants called bloomers while traveling by wagon. It was easier to walk—and safer!

bloomers

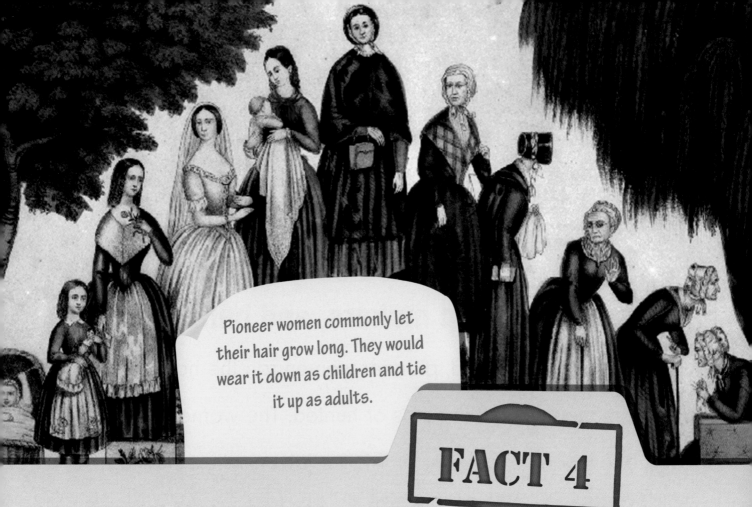

Pioneer women commonly let their hair grow long. They would wear it down as children and tie it up as adults.

FACT 4

Women on the **Oregon Trail** liked to wear moccasins.

Many women wore out their boots while walking beside the wagon. They traded with Native American tribes—or paid about $1—for the soft, **durable** moccasins along the way.

Women's Work

FACT 5

Frontier women worked as gardeners, cooks, laundresses, soap makers, and babysitters.

On their homestead, pioneer women ran the household, while the men worked in fields or hunted. The women of an area often worked together on bigger jobs, such as making bed covers called quilts. These helpful gatherings were called bees.

Not only did women do the laundry, they had to make the soap used to wash clothes!

Since there were few doctors, frontier women treated fevers, coughs, and illness without them.

Pioneer towns with doctors were often far away from homesteads. Women learned to use herbs to help the sick. Some **remedies** worked. Others, such as rubbing the chest with goose grease for a chest cold, didn't.

Pioneer women traded for new clothing.

The sewing machine wasn't widely available until the later 1800s. So, women often sewed clothes by hand. They commonly made their own cloth, too! Women also swapped clothing to "rework," or make new pieces from it.

Once towns were better established in the late 1800s, pioneer women were able to buy cloth more easily to make clothing.

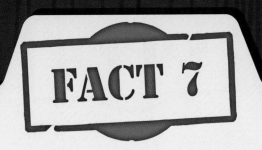

Clothing of a Pioneer Woman

bonnet: worn outside to keep the sun and wind off a woman's face

shawl: worn in cold weather

dress: commonly made of cotton or wool and made in a dark color

apron: worn to keep the dress clean

shoes: flat, made of brown or black leather

Pioneer women wore long dresses during the mid-1800s. They were usually fitted close to the body on top with a full skirt and long sleeves.

About 25 percent of white American women had been a teacher at some point in their life by the 1870s.

As more families moved west, more teachers were needed.

Teaching was commonly a men's profession, and women were

paid less for the same work.

Married women weren't allowed to be teachers.

Men greatly outnumbered women on the American frontier. As women moved west to fill the growing need for teachers, they were also filling the need for wives. However, once married, women had to leave their teaching jobs.

Special teaching colleges opened in the eastern United States for women to learn the job.

At the Homestead

FACT 10

Weddings were happy occasions, but they weren't just about love.

Men needed wives who could have children and handle the labor it took to run a frontier household. Women hoped for a skilled man who would work hard to support their family.

Frontier women ofter helped their husband in the fields in addition to household work.

One pioneer girl wrote that she milked 20 cows in 1 day!

Pioneer children had chores to do. Girls would watch younger children, do laundry, milk cows, and help their mother cook and clean. Similarly, older boys helped with their father's work.

Laura Ingalls Wilder

Laura Ingalls Wilder was born on the American frontier in Wisconsin. She wrote about her life as a pioneer in a book series, beginning with *The Little House in the Big Woods.*

A pioneer woman could go months without seeing anyone but her family.

Pioneer women were often lonely because neighbors lived far away. When communities met for picnics and dances, it was a big deal! These sometimes followed work such as **barn raisings**, too.

Women on the frontier loved to read magazines.

Pioneer women looked forward to the weekly mail. Newspapers and magazines connected them to the rest of the country and gave them stories to read. However, they had to go into town to pick it up!

During the mid-1800s, serials were very popular. Serials were stories that were printed one part at a time in magazines, such as *Harper's*.

FACT 14

Pioneer women heading to California traveled over two mountain ranges in a dress!

The journey to California was months longer than that to settlements on the Great Plains. The pioneers had to cross both the Rocky Mountains and the Sierra Nevada.

The last stretch of many pioneers' journey was about 40 miles (64 km) of desert near the California border. Some didn't have enough food and water left to cross it.

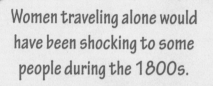

Women traveling alone would have been shocking to some people during the 1800s.

Women mined for gold during the California gold rush, too.

Like their fathers and husbands, pioneer women were excited by the idea of gold in California. While 95 percent of miners were men, some women traveled to goldfields *without* men altogether.

Luzena Wilson sold a homemade biscuit to a miner for $10, which is more than $250 today.

Miners really missed the work women commonly did during the 1800s. Some women made a fortune washing clothes and cooking—and never setting foot in a gold mine!

Women used their homemaking skills to make a living during the gold rush—and many ended up with gold of their own!

Women came to California from all over the world during the gold rush, including France, Peru, and China.

French girls charged an ounce of gold if a man wanted to simply sit next to them!

Only about 800 women lived among the 30,000 men in the California mining area in 1850. So, a woman's company had great value.

By 1857, women made up about half of the people heading to California. Towns such as Sacramento, California, grew from mining settlements.

FACT 18

Some women dressed as men to make more money doing jobs in California.

Elsa Jane Guerin lived as "Mountain Charley" while she worked as a **prospector**. When she made enough money, she went back to her children in St. Louis, Missouri, as herself.

FACT 19

Like many pioneer women, the famous Calamity Jane started her life in the West on a wagon train!

Martha Jane Canary, or Calamity Jane, was born in the 1850s. She could shoot and ride as well as any man and performed in Wild West shows in the 1890s!

Calamity Jane truly showed the independence of a frontierswoman.

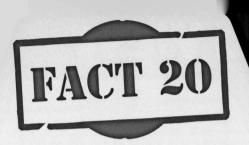

FACT 20

Pearl Hart was an early voice for women's rights.

Hart was known as the "bandit queen" for robberies she'd committed. When she was caught, she said she wouldn't consent to be tried by laws women didn't have a voice in making.

The women of the Wild West, such as another "bandit queen" named Belle Starr, challenged the position of women on the American frontier—and the law!

Pioneer Timeline

1803

The United States gains about 828,000 square miles (2,145,000 sq km) of land in the Louisiana Purchase.

1804

Explorers Lewis and Clark set out to learn about the new western land.

1810

The first person travels what will become the Oregon Trail.

1836

The first wagon train sets out on the Oregon Trail.

1846

An agreement with Great Britain adds new territory to the northwestern United States.

1848

The United States gains southwestern lands from Mexico, including California. Gold is found in California.

The pioneers were part of the westward expansion of the United States, or the growth of the country to the west.

27

Strength on the Frontier

Pioneer women had hoped heading west would bring them a better life. However, during the mid-1800s, the small homes of pioneers were far from neighbors and towns. They didn't have much, and there was always something that needed doing. Some families didn't stay more than a few years because it was so hard.

Nonetheless, all these women crossing the American frontier were true pioneers. They showed strength, bravery, and an ability to take on whatever came their way.

PIONEER WOMAN

barn raising: a gathering for the purpose of building a barn

durable: able to last

frontier: a part of a country that has been newly opened for settlement

historian: someone who studies history

homestead: the home and land received from the US government

laundress: a woman who washes clothes

legal: having to do with the law

Oregon Trail: a pioneer route to the northwestern United States

perseverance: the act of continuing despite hardship

prospector: someone who searches an area for valued resources, such as gold

remedy: a treatment of illness

For More Information

Books

Kravitz, Danny. *Surviving the Journey: The Story of the Oregon Trail.* North Mankato, MN: Capstone Press, 2015.

Russell, Greta. *Olive Boone: Frontier Woman.* Kirksville, MO: Truman State University Press, 2014.

Websites

The Oregon Trail
www.america101.us/trail/Oregontrail.html
Learn all about those traveling the Oregon Trail and the historic sites you can still see today.

Pioneers
www.kidskonnect.com/subjectindex/16-educational/history/276-pioneers.html
Find out more about the pioneers, and use links to learn more about this time in American history.

Index